My Experience

JACQUELYN HESTER COLLETON-AKINS

Ilustrated By:
Mark Ruben Abacajan

To order additional copies of this book, contact:
Xlibris
1-888-795-4274
www.Xlibris.com
Orders@Xlibris.com

My Experience

JACQUELYN
HESTER
COLLETON-AKINS

Illustrated By:
Mark Ruben Abacajan

The family went to bed with happy thoughts, thinking about my first day of school tomorrow. I woke up early, ate a big breakfast and put on my new school clothes. My aunt came and picked up my sister and brother and took them to school. My mother took me to school at Oceanway Elementary School. When we arrived at the school my heart was full of joy because it was time for me to start school for the first time. On my first day at Oceanway Elementary School, my mother took me to the office to register me for the 1st grade.

I saw other boys and girls my age in the office getting registered for the 1st grade. I asked my mother, "Do you know my teacher's name? She replied, "No I don't know." The lady in the office took my mother and I down this long hallway to the classroom #8. I saw a lady in the classroom door that greeted us with a kind smile. She turned around and said, "Well, you must be Jacquelyn". "I am", I said. The teacher spoke again, "Welcome to the 1st grade." "You will know your classroom the red door and a number eight on the door".

She introduced herself as Mrs. Bell. Mrs. Bell took me by the hand and led me to my seat. At my seat, I looked around the classroom at the other students. Everyone seemed nervous too. My mother waved good-bye and walked backed into the long hallway, and then she was gone.

Mrs. Bell asked me to tell the class my name. I was so afraid to speak when I opened my mouth, no sound came out. It was frightening because, I was the only African American student in the class. I didn't know what to expect from my new environment. When the bell sounded for us to go to lunch, Mrs. Bell asked everyone to get in line. Nobody wanted to be in front of me or behind me so I had to walk at the end of the line by myself.

During lunch the food smelled and looked so delicious. I got my mind off of how I was being treated by the white students; I stopped my mind from concentrating on the negativity and begin focusing on the positive things and focused on enjoying my lunch. My classmates was seated at the table eating together while I was sitting at another table by myself with no one to communicate with. Suddenly, I felt spagetti, meatballs, and chocolate milk landed on me. I felt like the whole world landed on me but I quickly braced myself remembering what my grandmother and my daddy taught me to turn the other cheek. During recess none of the students didn't talk or play with me. This experience made me felt all alone.

When the class returned from lunch and recess, I began working on my class assignments; my eyes kept gazing at the clock praying for three o'clock to come. School finally ended at 3:00pm, the bell rung to signal that school was over. I got up quickly from my seat and hurried to the door and Mrs. Bell said, "I enjoyed having you in my class and I look forward to seeing you tomorrow, "I said, thank you good-bye Mrs. Bell." While I was walking in the hallway, some students spit in my face, threw a cup of urine in my chest, and called me names (coon and nigger). I arrived at the front doors of the school and I saw my mother standing there with her arms open and I ran right to her arms. I tried to say something but my mother said, "calm down, calm down, calm down, you don't have to talk I understand what you went through on your first day of school". Baby you still look beautiful in your new clothing.

While walking home with my mother, some student's parents told us not to walk on the sidewalk. They said, "the sidewalk is only for white people not niggers", so walk in the street". My mother and I obeyed them and walked in the street. When we arrived home I ran up the steps and ran through the door yelling for my grandmother and I ran to my grandmother bedroom. I began telling her about my experience at school, but she just grabbed me and hugged me telling me she loved me and I had to go back to school tomorrow and for a whole year. Later that night I ate dinner, I didn't eat very much I was very quiet at the dinner table and I asked to be excused from the table to go to my room and when I got to my bed I felt like writing in my diary about the horrible things that happened to me. My grandmother asked me for my clothing so she can wash them but the stains never came out. I said to myself, "I will keep this outfit for motivation and strength".

Later that night my daddy came home and woke me up and gave me a hug and told me he loved me, Jacquelyn you must return back to school tomorrow. My daddy said let's get down on our knees and pray to Jesus to give you strength, knowledge, and wisdom to endure your trials and tribulations all because of slavery, for integration in the public schools. When I woke up the next morning I felt revived, and I felt like I had matured in a grown up way.

On Monday morning I walked into my classroom and I saw a girl who was a new student in a wheel chair, she looked nervous and afraid. I walked over to her and introduced myself to her and she introduced herself back to me and I saw that the kids were picking on her but her skin was white like theirs.

We became friends immediately, because she was going through what I was going through. I finally had someone to be seated by me in class, in lunch, and during recess. Four days passed and I found inspiration deep down in myself I loved school. I also found out I really liked my class and classmates. I have a friend named Shannon. Mrs. Bell told the class to call each person by his/her name. Mrs. Bell gave us name tags to fill out and to wear for the whole year. This procedure would enable the students to learn their classmate's names.

In class, Mrs. Bell gave a very special assignment for us to complete for homework. Our homework assignment was to write a story about one member in the family. I wrote a wonderful story about my great grandmother George Ann. The next day we had to read our story to the class. I was so happy to read my story to the class because during slavery time George Ann became one of the first African American teachers. After everyone read their story Mrs. Bell gave all the students an A+ for reading our story and doing a great job.

The school year passed by so fast, now it's time for summer we have three weeks left before school will be out for the summer. I will miss going to school everyday and being with my friend Shannon, and being in Mrs. Bell class. On the last day Mrs. Bell passed out the report cards I opened up my report card with joy and excitement because I only received A's and then I saw the big two, 2nd grade for next school year. The bell rung and Mrs. Bell said, "time to go home for the summer". I walked out the school and began walking in the street I did not care about walking on the sidewalk

then I reached my home my grandmother, mother, daddy, brother (Robin) and sister (Gloria) standing on the porch they began to clap their hands as I approach them and all of them embraced me.

I showed my daddy my report card and then he hugged me.

showed my mother my report card she hugged me.

showed my report card to my grandmother, brother, and sister and they hugged me.

My mother said, "lets go inside and eat some cake and ice cream" , and all of us was sitting around the table eating cake and ice cream.

The End

Afterword

In 2017, Jacquelyn is still having to fight for systemic racism, because everyone needs equal rights or equal protection of the laws in the United States of America.

Grade Levels: Kindergarten through 12th grades.

Characters

1.   Jacquelyn Hester Colleton-Akins
2.   Peter Hester (Daddy) – Deceased
3.   Ruby Hester (Mother) – Deceased
4.   Mrs. Bell (Teacher) – Deceased
5.   Shannon (Friend) – Deceased
6.   Robin Hester (Brother) – Deceased
7.   Gloria Hester Shepherd (Sister)
8.   George Ann Hester (Great Grandmother) – Deceased
9.   George Ann Hester (Grandmother) – Deceased

10.   Alice Hester (Aunt)

About the Author

Jacquelyn Hester Colleton-Akins, she is a minister and pastor for Jesus Christ, Educator, Nurse, Author of books, Physical Therapist, Mother, and Grandmother. She dedicated her life working with mentally handicapped students, cerebral palsy, autistic, gifted students, ADHD students, and ESOL students. She dedicates over 175 hours a week toward working with the older population with severe and moderate disabilities. She works with students has dropped out of school with bipolar conditions needs to be on medication. She provides food and clothing for the homeless, the sick, and the shut in that can not leave their home. She provides help for African Americans and Mexicans by helping them file charges for being discriminated on his/her job.